honor card & other poems

betsy colquitt

honor card & other poems

betsy colquitt

saurian press · box a · new mexico tech
socorro, new mexico · 87801

Acknowledgment

My thanks to the editors of the following anthologies and journals who accorded first publication to many of the following poems and who have graciously allowed the reprinting of these writings in this collection:

Southwest: A Contemporary Anthology, Red Earth Press
The Texas Anthology, Sam Houston State University Press
Fiction and Poetry by Texas Women, Texas Center for Writers Press
New and Experimental Literature, Texas Center for Writers Press
Texas Stories and Poems, Texas Center for Writers Press
Approach
Christian Century
Crucible
English in Texas
Forum
New Laurel Review
New Mexico Humanities Review
Pawn Review
Pilgrimage
Quartet
Riversedge
Sam Houston Literary Review
Sands
Vanderbilt Review
Vision

To Jerry Bradley, John Rothfork, and Jim Corey, editors of Saurian Press, I express my gratitude for their many courtesies and for their wise counsel about this collection.

Betsy Colquitt
Fort Worth, Texas

Cover photo by John D. Shortess

CONTENTS

A Prefatory Note

After moods, influences, groups and movements sweep time and again over the landscape of American poetry from decade to decade, what we prize, I think--what I know I prize--is the singularity of isolated poets as we see them once the dust has cleared. Reading closely, we begin to adjust to angles of vision, patterns of vowel and consonant, the syntactical dance: all those peculiarities that give the writer his true identity. Reading more closely still, we share that identity and return from our reading altered or shaped by it.

In Betsy Colquitt's poems such individuality is present--not part of the time but in virtually every poem, clearly marking every line here as hers. The subjects of her poetry are those most of us are familiar with and they range from family, aging and death to reflections on figures out of history or legend. For someone used to reading contemporary poetry, as I am, the most immediately striking feature of Mrs. Colquitt's poems is the vigorous independence of her style and the authoritative voice speaking there which creates and sustains it; they are quite unlike any poet's I can think of. Noticeable at once is her strong attraction to a vivid, muscular, and never ordinary diction: there is no catering to our latter day predilection for the dull, colorless or flabby word; instead, we need to reread lines occasionally to see just how words or phrases have been freshly employed; sometimes we are sent to the dictionary. This considerable (and carefully considered) range of language is matched by demanding arrangements of sound and syntax and by a terseness and elliptical manner that keep rein on any pull towards over-ornateness. Often enough, Mrs. Colquitt dispenses with the routine road-guides of punctuation--or anyway some of them--and so compels the reader to greater attentiveness and to a more accurate sense (on tongue, in muscles and nerves) of the way in which her lines and stanzas move. I·find, in this respect, much pleasure on a third or fourth reading of a poem in simply following a passage here or there for the beauty and accomplishment of its music, the steps of its rhythm. This, for instance, from "goya, his matador":

> *it's the eyes you see*
> *he saw*
>
> *that see the decades*
> *of bullfighting done*
>
> *leaving him witness*
> *to truth of thousands*
> *of bloodlettings,*
> *the beasts, his own...*

Or another stanza, chosen at random, which opens the lovely "bells of ireland":

> *In a field I find them--*
> *bells of Ireland, perfect*
> *graduated as carillons*
> *stems straight as aspens,*
> *and their colors are hers, reds*
> *bright as cardinals in prime*
> *and luminous as fine glass.*

In Betsy Colquitt's poetry her perceptiveness, wit, deep feelings blend with her extraordinary and individual sense of language and style. The personal signature of her art is an elegance and strength which is all her own, the product, no doubt, of much laboring, as Yeats said it must be. I hope many readers will discover these fine poems and attend to them with care, be moved and enlarged by the acuteness and the richness they embody.

Ralph J. Mills, Jr.
University of Illinois
at Chicago Circle

part one

photographing the facade
san miguel de allende

They are eternal as angels and demons.
Wrapped in clothes gladly rags,
offering for coins their antique hats,
they wait as they always wait,
these same beggars everywhere

at every church we visit:
the gaunt Indian mother nursing
a gaunt baby, the archetype
of lameness, and one whose flaying flesh
is rebus of pain.

A few miles away the freeway runs,
motels transmogrify the landscape,
and even on this square, plastics
and polyesters conquer market
where American Express buys us everything.

Yet these who waited surely
for Cortez before monuments
to other gods are constants,
and we who would take the facade
aim polaroid high; tilt viewfinder

to seek Saint Michael, putting down
a pink and wounded stony demon
and triumphing as he always must;
frame from film these wounded
lingeringly as Satan, as Christ

in some eternal and relentless scheme
that none of us does fully cause,
cannot resolve, and embarrassed
of irresolution, we search
with narrow focused eye
for Gothic things.

the lie and truth of this land

It's been tricky getting here: starting
basically with no directions, we circled
left and right through cul-de-sacs
in icy and fierce geographies.

Bonded, trothed, we foraged separately,
each army wanting provender and uncomfortable
in bivouac. Von Clausewitz too we left uncut
fooled of fickle, rare Corinthian weather,

and when our armies met, war was guerrilla.
You were good at hiding even in bare land,
but I'd skills for ferreting your defenses,
seeking keenly in private terrains.

Your tactics ran too often to waiting,
and I was primed always to quick muster,
knives bone sharp, thrusts apt to cold jungles,
though some victories tasted like defeats,

the cooking sad after butchering,
and our incisions festering, we helped,
had to, each other in draining wounds.
While we circled with meager compass

fretting northward, children sniffled
edgy of battleground, parents cheered
our skirmishes, friends, they laughed:
and after campaigns, usually on weekends,

there were Mondays to be got through:
work, school, grocery, money-changers
intruding preemptorily enough:
if compass couldn't guide, necessities did:

do: it would be nice to think the battles over,
jungle clothes for arctic guerrillas
packed with permafrost away, cul-de-sacs
mapped straight as interstates. They're not:

any moment compass will explode, spin expiry
to our brief order, terrain invite us
guerrillas to maiming though
less we respond to these invitations.

If we've staked no south fields
bountied of gentle flowers,
more now other unnorthern needs avail:
we're less proud, having been

often wounded, much defeated,
and I at least am afraid of the cold.
I'm weary of wrong compass, battle weather.
If not love, it's more love than hate.

and most days I'm amazed at our arrival,
come by circles, foolish turns,
icy, dulling combat to this tricky place,
the lie and truth of this land,

Corinth lust beyond deceiving tundra
our armies mainly easy at armistice
and rarely foraging, commissaried now
mostly from home.

two on gulliver

---

mrs. gulliver at home in newark

She managed well her years of waiting,
this Mary Burton, second daughter
to Edmond, hosier in Newgate Street.

Though homing carried comforts,
it had work, mysteries enough as she coped
with debtors, moves, children,

his absence, no letters coming
from worlds beyond posting -- and with him
home, these returns hardest, the voyages,

effects untranslated by her vocabularies.
His first trip back, he fondled her
like a kitten, a doll, kept wanting her

to walk on his hand, find the sheep tucked,
he said, in his pocket. After second trip,
he shouted each day her grossness,

then crept to her breast like a babe,
frightened by night, by sound of wrens,
terrified of the circus monkey.

After the third voyage, was he mad
she wondered, talking of sunning cucumbers,
of living forever yet yearning death,

demanding her beside him every night
to leave her in late pregnancy
and fly to captain mutinous ship.

When he came back smelling of horses,
in amity only with stallions,
she kept to duties, tended her children,

fearful of whinnying father. At first
she'd have dressed like a groom
to talk with him, to comfort this Yahoo,

but he'd no speech for her, and she thought,
came to think, her world worth her probing,
navigation treacherous, navigator unexplored.

After making meals, lessoning children,
she turned bookish, kept a journal, wrote at poems,
came hardly to note his whining, snuffy swoonings,

and finally grew impatient for his homing
to horses. She discovered this new country,
its solitude, self requiring little dialogue,
no voyaging to fit his farfetched worlds,

and even when Stella called with talk
of the curious Dean, best moments were
after, hours left to her jottings,
to quiet, her feathery bed singly quilted.

gulliver stabled

Finally his reason knew no limit,
learning from Emanuel aborted,
common sense deserting him

apprentice now to horses.
Thus returned to Newark,
he berthed in stable, forsaking

ancients and moderns to write tale
no one believed, neither Mary
nor his fearful children. Speaking only

with stallions, his speech at last
the nasals of Houyhnhnms,
he held to his flaying vision,

knowing such flaying altered him,
all appearance for the worst.
Fierce indignation tearing his heart,

he held to ironies too, the envelope
with lock of her hair,
and locket engraved *cogito ergo sum*
enfolding miniatures of his children.

Credulous, a gull fishing geographies
uncharted on any map, he did as he could,
his manifest invoicing terrible epiphany
of all perverse in his upright heart.

Sometimes late in night, measuring
with two sights of pelorus,
he thought on misanthropy,
wondered at topographies of pride,

thought of Mary, Captain de Mendez,
toyed with cartographies kinder
than reason and explored, compass
fixed to lover's cold star.

But nothing came of this.

Morning brought London and all its slops,
news of Vanessa dead, Stella ill,
the Dean melancholy and traveling
to madness, eyes now merely distorting.

Stabled he held to yieldness vision,
this sanguine man to whom misanthropy
wasn't indigenous and who should in reason
know hate briefly as singular fruit
of swift and deciduous season.

home economics: a marriage poem

we signed up with high hopes
that mayday. no signals sang
distress though early
june showed our economics unmelding.

you believed categorically
in the invisible hand, sweeping,
washing cups, smoothly oiling
what smiled in our market place.

and i leaned Keynesian,
deficitly spending disaffection,
stocking heavily in fool's gold,
yet yearned to buy realty of home.

you named this too your destiny
though your methods required wealths
only nations provide, and my principal
was mortgaged at too low interest.

such economies computed this argonne,
siege city in these Trojan walls,
our Gettysburg where daily you outflank
me. i'm inflated, you depressed

with our gross markets, high war profits.
my visible hand would scorn its pyrite,
and you want, convince me you do,
smithing better than your forgery

of Adam. these home economics
need all domestic science to allay.
yet mayday has, can have, other meaning
than distress, my friend, and i distressed

call you, your help, our help, call
my friend, my little friend.

to philomena uncanonized

"Philomena's official demotion finally came as part of a long-term program . . . to tidy up the liturgical calendar." Time

we who named you saint
unsaint you; born of our history
we unhistory you. never sturdy
like Theresa, noising
on Avila's discalced stones,

or Catherine, evangeling strident
in Siena and exiled Avignon,
you had no tongue
nor even tapestry
to tell your story.

bones were your only plot
though you sourced, quietly it's true,
miracles enough: healings,
visions, of which nuns wove
your uncloistered fame.

now expunged, lacking myth,
you grave in secular casket
friendless of clerics
and cautious laymen, perhaps though
saint and friend yet of God,

constant above his images,
embarrassed in our hasty christening
of your old statues and fast
dyeings of your glassy myth,
even as he knows now and always

true legend and your holy ghost
whose worth adds its light
to wax, quietly as candle
timeless and unflickering,
securely amid his own.

street child: ciudad acuna

I have been seeing him
as he has me
all our years:
boy slight, eager-eyed,
dirty hands holding Chiclets
that will metamorphose to shoeshine kit
and then to trays with jewels
of paste and metal
too greenly fraud for belief;

and I, gringo bringing money,
come daily to barter in border town
for crafty bargains, dropping silver
in soiled hands and seeing quaintness vanish
as greed coils fingers like snakes
and spirit gluts itself
on the sacrament of coins.

This our brief encounter occurs
as we are cornered by frenzy
of horns and cars, deadly as bullets,
racing the weekend streets,
and momently together in peril
we wait, I the American glutton for goods
and he the street child selling --
or so roled we seem

The view is existential, and home
tomorrow and putting away my gains,
I will think of none of it,
yet some vision intrudes of exchange
better than our trading
and of words that could have tongued
more than our cheap mutual defrauding.

french and france

charlotte benard, tutor

You won, you know,
and you'd be pleased.

Those long afternoons of supposed French,
you were of course schooling them,
your fortunate heirs,
my daughters,
but in something other than language --

rather in a lover's demesne,
its cartography
as lasting as mystery of sources
and as absent from being
as you since your heart's revolt.

And this summer,
their first journey in your land
they travel most your mappings:
Charlemagne yet kings generously,
always mindful of honor and Roland:
and William, conqueror never bastard,
commands your bony kin
to craft him sturdy towers.
In Burgundy, yield of ancestral vines
stills to dark wines delectable
beyond nectar, and chocolates
(casual of cavities,
you filled girls with these)
softer than butter, better
than highest cuisine.
wait in shops
rich as your foretelling.

What I see and show them, they see
and polite, these daughters,
do not dispute. But vivid
beyond vista of this transient summer
is your sweet France,
in transformation so splendid
it could exist (and did)
only in memory,
yours selective as kindest lover's.

You'd be surprised at how well
you taught and how faithfully
they learned your lessons --
not verbs or vocabulary
but your real subject, to which
you guided them by maps
surer than Michelin's.

And I watch, discomfited at my schooling:
a practicum of frenzy beyond staking
any demesne by memory of love:
and envy you those late afternoons
when you won them
and won for them this winsome country
grammared in beauty
and syntaxed by claim of love
sacred and legended as Roland's.

vacationers at amecameca

A clear focus we wanted,
so guidebook guided
we left the flowery market
to climb the sudden hill
remarking the rocky stations
of the Indian as Christ,

remarking too the pilgriming,
the old signing their Sunday black,
young in white or gaudy
as violent rainbows.

From the top, we said,
we would see volcanos unclouded
and we visioned how their snows
would reign on the high sky

but saw in fact only this site

shrine housing him who
we guessed
had once walked the hill
in message they accepted
and would hear preached again
by body secure in crystal tomb
and brown as dried leaves
noisy in demise.

The hill we'd read
is famous for its view:
we came for this
but at crest found only relic
whose lore we couldn't hear
and saw only seeming snow
of volcanos we knew easterly
but could not for clouds see.

helen unlored

One moment there
must have been
brief by its brightness
before desire despair
knowing terrible beauty
before they who saw
and she who was
knew and reckoned
as they must
her fatherhood of God
and brotherhood to man

before the drama was
from which legend came
that uncomprehending
we can neither ignore
nor forget.

One time at least
there must have been
before the lore began
when perhaps even she
was graced in innocence
favored by only loveliness
far away the day
when old men at Troy
would walled in wisdom
remark her beauty
counting beauty's fates,

a time when no reckoning
seemed needed
and beauty was attended
by nothing else at all.

traveling the outback

He's only modestly a dog,
no bigger than a cat,
and comfortable in petness.
Yet dreaming he's something else:
lying sidewise on my bed,
he imagines wildness.

Inch ants, beetles,
galah cockatoos demand his discipline.
Emus need chase.
His sleeping feet move miles
over hot Outback sand.

Dingos scare, baying in longing
toward desert moon,
and wild camels rushing our camp,
he shelters under bush
stickered as blackberries
to save its hard-won yield.

Hunting desert rats, he's more success,
his reality of mouse
triumphantly transformed,
and growl from his gluttonous throat
heralds sweetest victory.

As springs creak,
he yearns for springs,
the curious wells,
even sight of Indian Ocean.

Thirsty now, he whines himself awake,
passported in need to our mutual world
where outback is back yard,
and the only dingos near
pad in zoo eternity of cages.

As caged to me, he comes awake,
all wildness left in wilds,
and pet, he licks my hand,
and I give him his comforts,
water bowl, cellophaned jerky,
cakes of boney fiction, his dream

pristinely lost to this reality,
freedom's wiles and most fears bartered
for these comforts to ease our prisoning.

waking to the late news

turning from dreamy reality,
i hear the midnight song-and-dance
of some 40s movie; see Betty Grable,
Dan Dailey frolic in black and white,
the living color fled.

then across their tapping, whitest
shoes, frames of their still lives,
the teletype brings words:
sleep riddled, glasses buried in cover,
my eyes lose/grasp letters
as the words tap away.

then comes boldest face proclaiming
MILLIONS MAY DIE --
STAY TUNED FOR MORE NEWS!

i cannot stay tuned, my strings
unstrung, eyes spangled
with this elegaic dancing pair,
our mutual 40s lost, its color
resurrected only as history.

tuneless, my years danced away,
i probe this celluloid shard
-- did i really dress like that?
wear a cheerleader's sweater?
did i bounce when i walked? --
but i do not stay tuned for answer,

for these millions who may, will,
i know, with only immediate catastrophe
missing. the legend i believe
long awake from any dream moving
to an MGM happy ending, as waking

turning to dream, always i sense
this presence tapping over Betty and Dan,
over all us millions, tapping with gravity
through our slippery hours
its dance of our Late News.

omnibus

---

the glimpse is only a minute:
i am driving past the bus
and i see her,

pink scarf tied under chin,
white hair an unruly halo
and her pose instinct with age.

she could be Rembrandt's mother,
but she isn't: is mine and alone
though the bus is ferrying many.

'i must reach her,' i say
'i must stay her loneliness,'
but traffic forbids,

and no message goes through to her.
'i'll meet her at a later stop,'
i say, applying no brakes.

sight commutes to pictures moving:
i see the conductor coming to her
with his guard-dog in silent barking.

she does not hear the dog
(the panes give him many heads),
hardly knows conductor seizing her fare

though -- so my movie continues --
her old pennies are enough
for transport to her stop.

movie still running, i plunge on
at my own speed. i know i will,
in fact, catch her bus some other stop,

but meanwhile, i'm so encircled by traffic
there's no way to go
save with its irrevocable motion,

and she goes on alone,
as perhaps she must,
to where the bus is taking her.

part two

museum scene: an *adoration*

Look you there, magus,
you farthest from the child
and kneeling, knees creaking
slightly it's true.

See, sir, toward the child
looking as to speak,
his face centered in light
and his countenance smiling
at you awkward in your posture.

Let the posturing go, sir,
and look to his comfort.
I would you would see
and word his ease at this stable,
beasts breathing warm on him
and arms of his mother crossing
gently to sure his limber back.

His eyes show well enough
he knows
as she doesn't yet
that afternoon
even to thirst and the spear.
But now
in the perspective of kind time,
chiaroscuro working its truths,
he has joy too his province,

and courtesy requires, sir,
that you, bone-tired
of your dubious journey,
look to more than knees
and see beyond pigments of paving
to him, centered in light
that focuses out to touch you.

antediluvian

Meteorology wasn't then perfected
nor was the weather
though bones surely foretold
and eyes scanning skies finally
must have found clouds.

Not though when he started,
this novice of arks
hammering under blue
improbable as always
and worrying clear desert nights
with his busy mitering.

Disoriented in dry violent world
by vision of violent waters,
he crafted gopher wood
to shape sufficient for safekeeping
and gathered to sanctuary enough
of earth and sky for paradigm.

Absurd as any Dane
he leapt to faith in floods
on soil watered only by mirages.
As camels, sweating, fly-troubled,
moved annoyed at his noisy carpentry
and neighbors mocked him, architect
of vessel anchored awkward on land,

his pure heart willed one thing
to which the amazing ark was witness.
Frivolous he must have seemed,
building desert boat, useless
as boats in bottles; and eccentric,
so far from other men
it's said he walked with God
angered of concentric multitudes;
and heroic, bargaining to save
what God despaired of keeping:

and human: the drunkenness
born of his visionary deeds
flooding his dry and salvaged world
to command in torment his long
last god-haunted days.

triptych

in the flemish room

Postcards don't much enlarge them
these miniatures of pain;
the oily flesh real enough for strigels

on these busy canvases telling whole
legends of their saints:
wheels spin, arrows pierce,

and the flaying, oh that's the shock,
knife really going through skin
and the skin beginning its tearing

to leave the red thing left panel
shows: eyes, though, are all the same
even if cross is means:

the startled look of saints,
'hast thou forsaken' seeks speech
through pigments centuries old:

their startle at pain perhaps
(reality always surprises),
more their startle that now is time

of their dying, perhaps to glory
the eyes say, yes, to be martyr
that is question, final mystery.

uccello's st. george: interpretation

He saw in proper perspective:
the St. George poised for dragon,
its fire at vanishing point
of its fierce impotence; and the lady,
serene though leashed to dragon
transfixed for agony.

38

Allegory by color too is proper:
George's green saying laurels
for the church; the dun, enormous beast
the pagan hordes; the white gowned lady
telling natural goodness
that sacraments may redeem by grace.

Possibly too there are other meanings:
Uccello, friend of the Medicis,
must have interpreted widely,
and possibly,
just possibly,
the lady leashed to dragon
is indeed a lady leashed to dragon:

serenity may be her mien
but manners change
and white stains easily:
her dragons are real
and the leash is as strong
as the sword and more binding:

and even if one unwieldy dragon
is gored, others hide over mountains
in smoky background curling fretfully
and no George can slay them all:

I can believe this lady, my lady,
leashed to dragons,
and I can believe too
leashes are stronger than knights,
than swords or sacraments of mail.

goya, his matador

it's the eyes you see
he saw

that see the decades
of bullfighting done

leaving him witness
to truth of thousands
of bloodlettings,
the beasts, his own:

no mysteries are left him
except eternal ones:

horns of the deadly
and death wounded
wounded him well enough
that he survived in a way:

and his eyes,
somber, wise, telling,

speak from dark palette
the true color of things.

cezanne and mont sainte-victoire

'the stirring climax of Cezanne's art'
-- Cezanne: The Late Works

yes, he did move a mountain,
this mountain, as stroke by stroke,
he raised its granite toward canvas.
years and years he worked

harder than housemovers,
his task bigger,
and his moving moved slowly,
so much to unlearn, learn.

early, foregrounds dominate:
axial almond trees, houses,
roads decompose; palette dead-ends.
then toward the end he was seeing

how to do it, paints become
pulley, brush steady for lever,
Egyptian mechanics working
even for mountain, sized beyond pyramid

and so indivisibly itself,
its integer demanded all
his wholeness. to move such mass,
he slowly learned

the angles to brush, surest ground,
the primary geography of Mary's color.
and when finally at the end
his vision moved the mountain,

he discovered the simplicity
of its innocent form -- whole, unquarried --
enduring in his holy victory,
its victory in his wholly enduring.

gloss

falling asleep over
'Falling asleep over the Aeneid'
I dream you resting aside me
suddenly companioned
in my bed.

I look you, patrician head,
lonely profile, eyes troubled,
and your convenient instrument
(we are prelapsarian as Eden)
unchallenged by my likes.

we talk you and I
of loves ancestors God
madness come of knowing
too much who exactly one is
and not liking the one.

a common plague we decide:
if heritage carries the disease,
so too is my new country,
so plainly frontier,
contagious with it

and histories long or short
all have abysms --
we agree in our easy talk --
mad sanity finds us in any locus
even beds feathery as gardens.

and I dream you comfortably,
turning you like pages
skin smooth as bond
body careless as loose quartos
mind scrutable as boldest garamond

and am startled hearing you say
'we've never met' (you're right:
except for the meeting of poems),
and swift as Aeneas urging
through shamming gates of ivory

you escape my dream
and I wake
to think you like all my loves,
fancy more than real, easy
only in horny conspiracy,

and unsleeping now
I turn abed to touch
like comfort
these anxious runes
of your chilly poems.

for xanthippe: praise

For you, Xanthippe, I offer praise:
recompense against ills centuries laid
upon your bourgeois aims, ridiculed
by Xenophon, gossiped in Alexandria
keen to scandal you Platonic goodwife.

If in fact Socrates proclaimed
that married to you he could then stand
anything, he spoke as Greek
poor in chivalry but rich in wit
to phrase such partial wiseness
as in philosopher's truth.

Tending children, knowing what food
ample to meal and when and where,
making places for sleep, carding
to clothing, these, all unlofty,
are requisite for welfare general

and private, allowing a few
the leisured evenings of philosophy,
its long symposia a quest
for fine and abstract holiness.
But neither noble nor holy,

housewifely code can never canonize
though I've known a few fair women,
all unremarked, martyred by these creeds
as fatally as by any gridironed
or hemlocked dying, and something

need remarking of you, making
what mundane order can obtain,
for enduring his moon-bound needs
and not, for caring to birth and after
your sons, and for unsuccumbing,

faced even with wedding to martyr.
I like to believe that shrew, if you were,
you had provocation and knew
by marriage to Socrates,
you had stood almost everything.

Though it's late and past recovery
of your good name, I offer for you
and your bourgeois virtues
these words,
my bourgeois and mundane praise.

dr. johnson's crocodiles

He is one of my sources
and I think of him often:
most by Boswell's lexicography
and sometimes by sources his own.

Words were his true source,
and language ways he knew firmly
though it's said knew
'not so much where the word came from
as what norms ought still
to be guiding':
thus his crocodile
swampy in etymology
as 'saffron-fearing beast.'

So seeing crocodiles
lazing at the zoo --
they are always lazing --
and graceless to become
their wordly fate,
I breathe to sluggish ears
their wondrous surprise
out of Dr. Johnson

and magically, suddenly swift,
syllable-shattered from sloth,
their wide teeth useless
and chattering like rabbits,
in tears now only for themselves,

they flee in flight before me
come of this lexical hour
to tell their fortune in saffron,
the changling vegetable gold,

and they discover themselves
transformed to sentience
by spell of word: these
once slumbering solid
and impervious as rocks

metamorphosed by news of crocus
to search on wide savannas
their mystery of being
fleshed by word.

# of some recent dead

1.

how do you Mister Death
like e e
cummings at you

coming with lyrics and loves
into your really enormous room
coming wide-eyed and word handsome
leaving legatees busied
computing his one-time equations
deciding on the tulips
of his puddlewonderful
and maybe periodless world

how do you like your blue-eyed boy
who waits
having even now perhaps
enough higher octane
of estlin
and in a way edwardian essence
to transform oysters to pearls
sweeping into your narrow realm,
        suited only to Cambridge ladies,
and ready to convert its missing all
into whatever Serene Illustrious
        and Beatific
if to be found by this Lord of Creation
Man

2.

Where walls fall and nothing gold can stay
your dying reminds us of all going
as ash not gold to perhaps yellow wood
after spring pools, snow fields and ways,
colts, tramps, masks, your old man's icy night
dark by your ironic displacing,
you having so well described this world
we think you'd move uneasy in any other.

And going now our miles toward sleep,
we, uneasy of pastures and runaways,
woods and desert places, are of you taught
landscape of lands we cannot escape
rich in terror as love, beauty as pain,
to mark wise the wry and frosty cautions
even as we learn there is in fact no stay.

3

Who traded in words wheelbarrows daisies
medicines is now beyond their barter.
Trips to contagious hospitals
booted no end of contagion
save for brief isolated cases
and no physician we know
can save finally or ever could

yet within inevitables
spanned spanking to life
comforting to death,
you patterned of Paterson
ways older than oldest Jerseys
citing some wholenesses
and many ails and woundings

now scribing and prescribing done
you leave what caduceus cannot wand away,
earthy lines mythy as Hermes
and assuaging by roots Horus cannot talon.

4.

to join these now
you come politic cautious meticulous
full of high sentences and no bit obtuse

decorously dying
in the London winter
to appropriate burial east of Coker

having come a long way
by whatever measure
from St. Louis
to greet the Eternal Footman
and learn now finally
of give sympathize control

as in our rooms
critics come and go
talking of Mr. Eliot so
bidding quick and troubled good nights
hurriedly because please
it's for us after all still time.

5.

how do you Mister Death
like these poets coming
still limbed
once life bright
world and wordly wise
having guised and smithed
sturdy kingdoms on doings
theirs/yours/ours
makers crafty
even in your enormous
day and/or night

republic **remembered**

He was right to distrust it:
poetry is a lie
not to be brought to truth
by makers' confessions
or exposed beyond narrowest limits
by scholars or craft of philosophers.
Like his cave, complete and postulant,
it sustains in metaphor
and by webs of words
lured to reel by limning.

He was right of course
to distrust and to spin
as argument contrivance
so obvious only philosophers
could believe it:
no poet or maker of beds
could find such sophistry
convincing.

Unlike poets, Plato I imagine
believed his metaphor
with only philosopher's part of brain.
The brain has many others.
Poets have as chief defense
how totally they are liars.

poetry and post, texas

out of a high school writing contest
what miracle is wrought
except a poet? whose land
is jackrabbits big as coyotes,
mesquites with china roots,
and dust bowling over dust
though sun lanterns
and stars lacquer the wide sky.

he's never seen a daffodil
nor does Pecos flow like Avon,
yet this marvelous boy manned of language
visions his landscape whole:

jackrabbits graced as unicorns
roam these lines
where mesquites laurel their prickly legend
and dust, sun, stars metaphor
his universe, full of bad typing,
worse spelling,
yet overcome by poetry.

sick of paltered lines
on paltry passions, I find
these lifting craft to heaven's gate
and ringing by his sight.

it's not enough to judge he's won:
he's by God a poet, and Post
and all West Texas
can never by proclaimed again
the same.

part three

program note

"I live in almost continual vexation, envy, and
persecution."   -- J. S. Bach

     I posture in my listening attitude,
     cup hand to face, ignore program's loss,
     watch him maneuver fingers, stops,
     feet to sound this

     the capellmaster wrote
     amid fathering; householding;
     churching as in Leipzig
     and teaching choir boys Latin;
     flattering nobles, the counts
     and kings; tempering well the clavier,
     fashioning Anna Magdalena her book,
     and making by deed our music

     amid vexation, envy, persecution.

     Amid vexing, envies, persecutions
     and persecutings, I can listen
     only unlisteningly, see organist
     move in time of sunbeams, playing fugues
     upon his form, and make of metallic blinds
     a kaleidoscope on walls,

     but make no music, nor words,
     nor love, nor life: nor know
     except for this
     half life of posture,
     as here of listening,
     always of doing,

     and observe myself restive
     look more earnest to the keys,
     wonder where to sup and if to sleep,
     and sharply note, relieved, program,
     tempered to better than my flat being,
     three-quarters through.

for frank, lost in the china sea

'How small a part of time they share
that are so wondrous sweet and fair.'

Like that Greek day
so I imagine
was his,
day of provisioning brightness
marked on earth
by full summering raiment
in the sky
by calm winds
all rudeness suspending

and beneath, smooth sea.

Like Icarus
he too felt triumph
so machined
as if wax-welded,
moving feather light
till fell mechanic trickery
made heavy the steel,
and wanton, curving,
plane revolted
to silvery spiral.

Instruments rioted
to proclaim the fall,
by numbers tell
brittle sea waiting
braking
for fragile craft
and brittle bone parcel.

A sliver sky-dropped
broke calm of surface
as gulls fish-scanning
roundly keened
a benediction.

Now in Texas season
gaudy with judas,
orchards in flame,
pears in communion dress,
I hear of that plunging moment

and would speak his Icarian
but unlegended descent
sharpening in blunt words
feelings not of kin-grief
but keen in loss of him
once student, then pilot and dead.

wonder if he who read
of warring heroes struggling
sirened seas was schooled
in whatever ways of poems
for his heroic fall;
if play of monarch battle
instructed for games of war
acted by blood and dyings;

hope the lyrics,
sweet sad jeweled songs
of fair young gone,
which he read most young and fair,
seemed prescient,
made time more dear,
offered comfort
in their uncomfortable words,

and that in time of falling
panic was not all his crew.

girls in the rain

Carrying shelter, they move carapaced
like swift turtles gaily shelled,
not huddled, these school girls,
but walking boldly their slippery steps
and nourished it seems
by rain they flee.

And from office view,
I who have noted their migratings,
confusing warblers touching in fall
to our falling world, watch
these of this season,
their umbrellas shell games
all win and lose.

Quick they come and go,
feeding in this field, this campus,
to find our knowledge wanton
and teaching by their presence
exempla of beauty to us
professing its abstracts.

In our words and nominal tone
they hear such madness .
as dooms Cassandras to frenzy
that they, so many Helens sheltered
in youth walled safe as Troy,
may in courtesy hear
but whose grave argument
they need not, now at least,
believe.

trees and progress

This is their last spring, these trees,
and untutored by hollow-eyed houses
with jacks as new foundations,
these soon to lie earth level
bud, their branches gold
in promise of this afternoon.

Borers, ants might have worded them
their doom. Progress too sends messages,
but not such as trees early hear,
and this afternoon
they stand apriled and foolish
brilliant in their confidence of June.

housebuilding

people who build glass houses
ought to have thought of the birds:
when walls of glass sit
so that from angles crows come --
soi-disant, no crows have crashed --
nothing opaque shadows
and birds hit hard these panes.

seeing familiars, trees, sky beyond
and innocent of vacuums,
they reckon empty this glassy space
that is our house
and come full flying
into the crystal sheet,
to bed on deck or ground,
bones so askew and feathers out
we sometimes don't know
who they are.

this has happened many times
and supports speculatives of sight
and sense and nature's ways and man's,
yet always I sorrow for these birds
unwary of our tricks with sand
and wish we could post
and they'd understand sign warning
Birds Beware or Glass, Alas!

housebuilding taught us much
of foundations, need for sealing
to slow the falling apart,
of water's inevitable flow
even through ground-level room;
but their crashing dying
is the most expensive knowledge --
emotionally that is --
housebuilding gained.

62

as with much else of wounding
and measured in pain,
I'd change our house
were it to do over
to darker and warmer place,
more hospitable for insight
and less inviting to injury
by its hard and optic illusions.

uses of nature

uses of nature are adverse and not
I am reminded by season and history:

winter barely festivaled
before quince, forsythia flower
celebrating garishly
this Lenten weather;
out of rocks weeds spin,
bulbs break green the ground,
sticks bud, birthed
in adversity and not,
born sometimes with our aiding.

history stories too of nature,
of man and nature.
because they are most omnipresent,
I think of sparrows and of some story
of sparrows and war,
of some warrior who doused
sparrows of China in flammables,
set flame, and loosed them
over villages he would take

and did, the burning birds
mad to flap flames out
dipping shortest way groundward
to bright to fire, then ash
straw of roof, yard,
houses, barns, people, children,
all like Medea's magic
a sorcery of inflaming.

uses of nature intrinsically
are both of birth and dying,
and nature is always adverse
and not: and man upsets
by too much of use either way.

I think of the burning sparrows
not as a Francis would,
such kinness removed and only visionary,
but as natural things undone
in wanton parable
of our woundings east and west

and feel, remembering vague history
in this season bursting to fullness
and almost rich enough
for sparrows rich in gluttony,
greeds, guilts of my own
and akin to my kind.

ducks at dawn

---

they storm this cold sky
in torrent of cloudy wings,
throats shrill as mad prophets.

lost to disorder, these hundreds
wanting compass purpose
wait direction as stilled

to circling, they skirmish
in combat with the characterless sky.
flying to no flight, they keen

their keening for right sight,
eye lined to slightest feather ahead
to direct isosceles of flight.

now current blind, treasoned
in this dubious season,
they spiral in the dizzy sky
and cry chaos at letterless dawn.

reduced circumstances

the barbering's skillful --
that can be said for it:
a lock gone there, a follicle here
sealed sure as tomb
against re-being; and the color,
brown gone white so goldenly
I hardly saw it:
eyes neither what they were.

all things considered
it's been a dexterous manicuring,
nails hardening at rates
beyond clear filing away,
and the muscle tone washed to fat
on shores of fatigue
so plush and sleepy
I never even noticed:

but I do:
random sight reflected
in department store window:
and am suddened to shock
beyond any buying
at how my credits are gone.

what happened
and when
that this is me:

debauched to reduction
in circumstances that optimist
I, always slouchy in spine,
could not on darkest day
have imagined:

and this day is bright.

cuptowels

hanging in the sun
their past comes through:
the feed-sack dye
of Plymouth rocks
cackling history
fabled as their being:

shrunk of their seeds
and raveled of three-thread seam,
sacks, washed and sunned
and appropriately lyed,
waited mothless cedared months
for translation to treasure:
prints to shirtwaists of copious hems
and to bonnets for babies
who might melt under the sun;
and the scraps whatever shape
saved to patchwork quilts
for millennial everydays:

domestics, though, still told
their tales through lye
that never quite worked
however vehement,
and their destiny,
plebian and inevitable
as drudgery neolithic to our day,
was cuptowels:

and these hang now
remnantly
amid my wash

telling of how one sycamored afternoon
swinging leisure of her porch
she bordered this sack cloth
with cross-stitch, appliqued
busy Dutch girls on, and almost
transfigured this native cloth
to fables of Netherlandish being
except for dyes of these triumphant hens
never quite purged from seeing:

now on clothes lines bedecked
with polyesters anonymous as detergents
these hens beyond all lyeing
parade as mighty shades
bloodless and real
over stitched and fabulous being,

and summon by their keening lines
marvel and life of all tumular story.

pronoun

lacking reference
and wanting antecedent,
I seek for nouns,
nomenclature for meaning
by which allusion
I gain definition;

look imperatively
within sentences
declarative
and interrogatory
and beyond,
backward too in old laws
of grammars, or forward
to some transforming scheme.

yet here I stand grammarless
caught in relentless present
progressing in tenseness,
undone by punctuating,
and in uninflected language
seek modifiers against law's threat
of composition in bankruptcy.

yet meaning is lost,
misplaced,
dangling useless as threads,
as tongues
mad at terror
and speaking from dry mouths
words no ears beyond this
I, lonely as a comet,
can hear,
nor even one intelligence
is compelled
by need or in compassion
to translate
or parse for meaning.

scene

Don't scream the dragonfly away
    stopping a moment busy wings still
    mounting my curious finger

He could as easily hold his blueness
    in flight arrested
    over crest of lawn or wave

You're right of course
    there are many dangers
    numbers of things to scream at

Don't ever my child
    be lured to cave or mountain top
    thinking dragons extinct

Though fire-breathing is outmoded
and daggering tails are cloaked
    dragons roam legion
    and no wise child thinks otherwise

But dragonfly is nothing for fright
    in our setting of alarums
    don't exorcise this gentle excursioner

Praise him rather in silence and sight
    delight in this quick blue vision
    which really and truly can't hurt.

part four

honor card

Five by seven, aged brown,
it confers in fine penmanship
privileges on Miss Eddie Young
for her good scholarship,
Spring 1902, McElhaney's Academy,
the academy a note now
in someone's history
of Major Erath's county.

She was bright and had good bones,
now gone to earth, and heavy hair
that lasted almost long enough,
and in 1902, too poor to stay,
left the academy
with contempt for her father
        who couldn't pay
        couldn't manage hen and chickens,
        squandered what little he made
        on books, only things he owned
        or wanted to, and read
        driving a borrowed plow
        on a rented farm.

And from the womb was angry
with her mother
        young wife birthing to season
        who widowed, dragged her brood
        to unwelcomes in ten spacious counties,
        and finally child-freed spent decades
        in someone's spare room waiting death
        to come like a dark bridegroom
        and he did and found her sleeping.

And fifteen, their firstborn,
she my mother left
whichever rundown farm
where cotton never made
    furrows what they were
    and weevils rampant
to work for money
selling in a general store
and buying there almost her wages:
    the gold bracelet delicately chased;
    apricot mull for dress so lovely
    it stayed sixty years unfading
    in her mind; and tortoise comb
    to become the lavish hair.

This of course is long ago
and finding honor card
of her abandoned school
in her death-abandoned house,
I conjure by this relic
this once girl
most recent to me old woman
who wheelchaired counted hour by hour
'one two three ten,' beginning again
a hundred times, knowing such numbers
get no honor cards
nor starting the alphabet with *k;*
who screamed at thoughts
meandering like a buried river
in terrain of her dying brain;
and cried at her one good hand
gauzed like a boxer's for her jerking
from her flesh
unwanted intensive cares.

Contemptuous of her pooring
        lavish beyond right heritage
and of her passiveness
        betraying her right character
and angrier at herself
than she ever was at anyone,
she tried again and again
to escape her paralyzed world,
restore brain to order, body to use,
but numbers were random
letters lost
and motion only dearest fiction.

And frustrated
she raged at this old woman
unable to please the ghost
of Mr. McElhaney or God
and certainly not herself.

I like to think her now
beyond rage, terror, tears
beyond forgiveness and forgiving,
turning young, light,
in raiment bright as apricots
soft as mull, her hair splendid
beside Berenice's, her wrists
supple and gauzed only by gold,

and in honor and God's grace
moving sure as stars
radiant as constellations
easy in Zion
and easy too in self.

recital

This new year's day I'm full of resolution:
today I take up the piano.
Hanon and Czerny will carry me back
to my thirteenth year, my stiff fingers,
rigid left hand turning supple as snakes.

My family fled to distant bedrooms,
I shall play the *Fantasy Impromptu* through.

It isn't easy: my fingers bend
to polishing silver, even subtle chases,
and to requirements of wools, delicate
at hand-wringing, but chromatics,
the first ones, stop me. I repeat

where there is no repeat. I repeat,
and bedroom doors close noisily above me.

And here in my living room
I try again: this time with a running start
my left hand almost makes it, rigid
third finger moving out of memory
as I summon up the curious legend
of fingering, where they go,
what the black keys require:

suddenly one door closed behind me opens,
I become her that I was
before hand-wringing was invented,
before silver knew any of tarnish,
the girl who conquered the two-part,
no, three-part inventions:

I am the girl in the pink net recital,
my petticoats taffeta soft beyond dream
my rose velvet sash perfect in its bow,
and my piece is last:

my freckles translate to flush
as in sweet hush of gardenias,
mildly askew on my shoulder
and waking the piano to fragrance,
I step in grace to the keyboard

just after Marybeth Wyatt's botched Beethoven
and Frank Demerson forgot *Kinderszenen,*

and with perfect touch of memory,
my fantasy soars
impromptu in this turning year
as above, behind, closed doors open, awed
by my sounding this mystery of resurrection.

after music, my father

After music it would be dusk
and he would be waiting me
freed from tyrannous keyboard
lysoled against my contagions,

freed from scoldings
by Miss Cross who stood
metronome wary, ruler in hand
under the languid Christ
companioned by Beethoven
deaf to my violations
she too keenly heard
and shamed like leprosy.

And dismissed
I would come running
through her garden
in rainbow of iris and crocus,

come in grief for rhythms
my measures could not reckon,
lamenting melodies locked
forever from my fingers,
awkward beyond deciphering
the misty code of Schirmer.
My parody of music mocked my ears,
and clumsy and unmelodious
I ran to him as to love.

And in the swift dusk
he waited innocent of Mozart,
untouched by Bach, unknowing of masses,
his only music one song, a whistling
his lips awkward as my hands
could not really make.

And turning from garden
where Miss Cross instructed me
'God walked' and I ran in terror,
my father and I drove
from my lesson long as dog days
through streets darkening by trees,
their trunks already nighted,
drove most securely home
in our innocence of this spring night

measuring his ending
to carry him,
gentle whistler of almost a song,
quickly irrevocably beyond home
beyond daughter
to whatever lessons of his long home

and abandoning me to lesson
longer and more scolding than music
and to searching always
as in frightening gardens
where there are -- must be -- messages
but coded fierce as Schirmer
and as beyond my deciphering
and where neither father nor God walks.

going with gravity

Our hill glitters
treacherous in its sheath
honed of this sudden storm,
and like some petty god
cornered by a warm haven,
I peer from house toward ice
and her who will go to school
down a hill no car
can take but to disaster.

I watch her unsure-footed
slide and fall,
books scattering like marbles
and cautiously redeemed
as she moves sidewise
against slope
turned shrill as Everest,
her familiar world coldly betrayed.

My vision fails her face
though I know its look
redding now to more than cold
and grotesque at awkwardness.

Then she begins again,
this time better,
and takes the slide
books in arms
going with gravity
and trusting inevitable fall
as much as Augustine, less sure
of grace than Francis.

And going beyond my sight
she slides still imperiled
but guarded by knowing learned
in movement that expectation
eases even inevitables,
and reckoning of puny forces
may suffice to break
if not to counter fall.

lesson: tom

I like the scene:
she's six, bewildered of worlds,
knowing and not knowing
bewilderment, possessed
enough to imitate at home
the worldliness of school:

on sister, at two
bewildered only unknowingly,
gay in haphazardy
much in control.

The lesson is reading:
list of words recited
none too exactly
by exacting instructress.

'Tom,' the student says
of all words;

'No, no, this word is Susan,'
teacher scolds.

'Tom, Tom,' the student proclaims,
knowing all words seen
as Tom now forever
and word without end.

I've heard her proclamation
so long I almost believe
all words like her Tom
a sacred syllable

and find this word like others
puzzle in letters I know
sounds I've heard
meanings I can comprehend

beyond comprehension
of letter sound sense

a curious pedagogy
bringing knowledge
of knowing no thing
nothing at all.

dream dogs

What beasts are these
come in black near morning
hounding you
from drowsy sheets,
your eyes suddenly wide
quick feet urgent running
in dark to my bed.

'Dogs' you say
plunging my way.

Turning this night
I've heard your turning,
restless then running,
my sleep bayed back
by beasts almost at heart
and good at dark pursuit,
tracing by scent
more subtle than blood

though nothing of four feet
hunts as my beasts do.

And waiting their charge
these ominous hours
I've watched the garden,
its jasmine silvering
under stingy moon
and its sweetness
standing against dark barks
stalking in groves of lawn.

Better than flower
as stand against dark
is your heavy sleep,
your head light on my arm
and staying till light
dark animals roaming
our nights,

my beasts bayed
and vexed almost beyond scenting
by the foul fiends born
of your six years' dreamings.

girls, after ceremony

Thicket separates drive their car comes
from where I hide seeking clothes
and listen as these girls arrive chattering
senseless as jays. Middle-aged
and familiar of grave ceremonies,
I know their camaraderie, survivors'
surprised laugh after last rites
that says of a contemporary's dying
'yes we endure, come safe from death simples,
skilled hiders from grave seeking.'

They're high school girls, this carload,
and death, swift mysterious, come
to one of them is new to them all:
to her this noon entombed,
to them witness to syllogism
that all girls are mortal
though non-Aristotelians, they're logicless
enough to feel still live, immortal.

Yet as they chatter, she touches them
and will, in dreams, in memory
when head turns a way they recollect,
as quick girl stoops to retrieve comb
falling from bright hair, when a laugh
sounds like one they can almost
place, and then placing,
they'll think her in her new place

and come to know how they lost
this noontime maidenhood more fragile
than hymen. Somewhere far back
in heart learning mortal marriage,
they'll hear her, saying 'yes you endure
a while, meanwhile I hide waiting darkly
seeking.' And some syllogisms
they'll discover persuade,
and even a generalization may be
particularly true.

I gather the dry wind-spun wash
to spindling basket and thread my way
to drive where she my daughter waits me.
I look to her come from first grave,
her friends now carred, carried away,
and will listen, try to answer whatever
it is she'll find herself unable to say.

pentecost

"And how hear we every one in our own tongue?"   -- Acts 2:8

Our neighbors talked with God
and every meal was Pentecost,
even least towhead shouting to ceiling
as flour gravy jelled to paste
and house cats battled devils.

At table before uncurtained window
they prayed through hungry summer,
sibilant tongues sounding meals
like muezzins, while in our house
table expected no guest of Emmaus.

Then sudden as they'd come
they fled the rented house,
mattresses a Jacob's ladder
ascending atop their car.
"To preach," my mother said,

"called to Pecos. Likely
they heard a jackass bray."
Easy mocking, she laughed watching
my father gathering from privet
their messy last leavings.

I gathered their leavings less easily.
Their God's ghost haunted, unfamiliar,
unanswered in my catechism,
and scared by their bold rejoicings,
worried at mother mocking

unchurched father, my unknown self,
was left confounding noisy mystery.
Only after years of unknown language
could I believe Whitsun touches clovenly;
that mother in candor mocking

and kindest father ordering, keeping
are ways of hearing even as neighbors,
their cats bedeviled, anciently heard
to shout above wherever Pecos;
could accept catechism as mystery,

counfounding need of self
praying only as silence,
listening to hear as absence,
and knowing best in unknowing,
all witness betrayed and clouded.

bells of ireland

In a field I find them --
bells of Ireland, perfect
graduated as carillons
stems straight as aspens,
and their colors are hers, reds
bright as cardinals in prime
and luminous as fine glass.

And I cut, cut, cut, scissors
snapping like turtles
as my arms stretch
to embrace these marvels
and I run flower-heavy
looking everywhere for her,
run beyond forsaken world
to garbled fields,
think myself lost falling
as from a steep yard
falling far to find her

and I do:
not amid spindly asphodel
but as once she stood
content
watching her flowers
ringing to spring.

She is not old
or sick or dying but young
and laughing at my odd blooms
born of dreams.
She reaches to my arms
no longer tired,
takes my dubious flowers,
and holds them easy in her spirit.

She touches my face, calm
with wonder
at her garlanded in love
and of world bright as prime,
sweet as light,
sudden as resurrection,

and at her touch I wake.

Biography

Betsy Colquitt is professor of English at Texas Christian University and has taught in the Writers' International Workshop at the Universidad de las Americas in Puebla. Editor of several books, including *A Part of Space: Ten Texas Writers,* she is also editor of *Descant.*